HALLOWEEN
PUMPKIN CARVING STENCILS

INSTRUCTIONS

PLACE A PATTERN ON YOUR PUMPKIN, THEN USE A PUSHPIN TO POKE HOLES ALONG THE LINES OF THE PATTERN. REMOVE THE PATTERN, AND CARVE ALONG THE LINE OF DOTS YOU CREATED.

THANK YOU A LOT FOR BUYING THIS BOOK. WE REALLY HOPE IT MET YOUR EXPECTATIONS AND THAT YOU ARE SATISFIED WITH THE PURCHASE!

WE WOULD REALLY APPRECIATE IT IF YOU LEFT A COMMENT AND A REVIEW ON AMAZON!

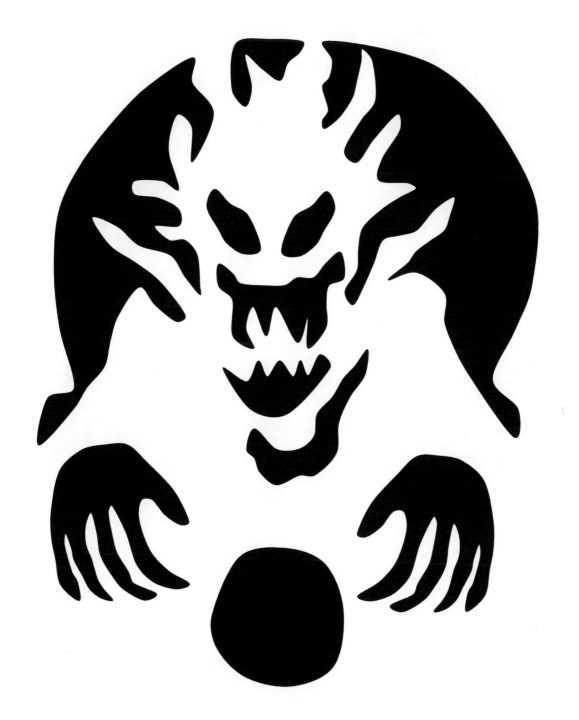